Seven Days of Fun

Weekly Planner for Kids

Activinotes

DAILY JOURNALS, PLANNERS, NOTEBOOKS AND OTHER BLANK BOOKS

Name: ....

Address: ....

E-mail: ....

Contact nos.: ....

....

Seven days of fun

MONDAY

TUESDAY

WEDNESDAY

THURSDAY

FRIDAY

SATURDAY

SUNDAY

NOTES

Seven days of fun

MONDAY

TUESDAY

WEDNESDAY

THURSDAY

FRIDAY

SATURDAY

SUNDAY

NOTES

Seven days of fun

MONDAY

TUESDAY

WEDNESDAY

THURSDAY

FRIDAY

SATURDAY

SUNDAY

NOTES

Seven days of fun

MONDAY

TUESDAY

WEDNESDAY

THURSDAY

Weekly Planner

FRIDAY

SATURDAY

SUNDAY

NOTES

Seven days of fun

MONDAY

TUESDAY

WEDNESDAY

THURSDAY

FRIDAY

SATURDAY

SUNDAY

NOTES

Seven days of fun

MONDAY

TUESDAY

WEDNESDAY

THURSDAY

Weekly Planner

FRIDAY

SATURDAY

SUNDAY

NOTES

Seven days of fun

MONDAY

TUESDAY

WEDNESDAY

THURSDAY

FRIDAY

SATURDAY

SUNDAY

NOTES

Seven days of fun

MONDAY

TUESDAY

WEDNESDAY

THURSDAY

FRIDAY

SATURDAY

SUNDAY

NOTES

Seven days of fun

MONDAY

TUESDAY

WEDNESDAY

THURSDAY

FRIDAY

SATURDAY

SUNDAY

NOTES

Seven days of fun

MONDAY

TUESDAY

WEDNESDAY

THURSDAY

Weekly Planner

FRIDAY

SATURDAY

SUNDAY

NOTES

Seven days of fun

MONDAY

TUESDAY

WEDNESDAY

THURSDAY

FRIDAY

SATURDAY

SUNDAY

NOTES

Seven days of fun

MONDAY

TUESDAY

WEDNESDAY

THURSDAY

FRIDAY

SATURDAY

SUNDAY

NOTES

Seven days of fun

MONDAY

TUESDAY

WEDNESDAY

THURSDAY

FRIDAY

SATURDAY

SUNDAY

NOTES

Seven days of fun

MONDAY

TUESDAY

WEDNESDAY

THURSDAY

FRIDAY

SATURDAY

SUNDAY

NOTES

Seven days of fun

MONDAY

TUESDAY

WEDNESDAY

THURSDAY

FRIDAY

SATURDAY

SUNDAY

NOTES

Seven days of fun

MONDAY

TUESDAY

WEDNESDAY

THURSDAY

FRIDAY

SATURDAY

SUNDAY

NOTES

Seven days of fun

MONDAY

TUESDAY

WEDNESDAY

THURSDAY

FRIDAY

SATURDAY

SUNDAY

NOTES

Seven days of fun

MONDAY

TUESDAY

WEDNESDAY

THURSDAY

FRIDAY

SATURDAY

SUNDAY

NOTES

Seven days of fun

MONDAY

TUESDAY

WEDNESDAY

THURSDAY

FRIDAY

SATURDAY

SUNDAY

NOTES

Seven days of fun

MONDAY

TUESDAY

WEDNESDAY

THURSDAY

Weekly Planner

FRIDAY

SATURDAY

SUNDAY

NOTES

Seven days of fun

MONDAY

TUESDAY

WEDNESDAY

THURSDAY

FRIDAY

SATURDAY

SUNDAY

NOTES

Seven days of fun

MONDAY

TUESDAY

WEDNESDAY

THURSDAY

FRIDAY

SATURDAY

SUNDAY

NOTES

Seven days of fun

MONDAY

TUESDAY

WEDNESDAY

THURSDAY

FRIDAY

SATURDAY

SUNDAY

NOTES

Seven days of fun

MONDAY

TUESDAY

WEDNESDAY

THURSDAY

FRIDAY

SATURDAY

SUNDAY

NOTES

Seven days of fun

MONDAY

TUESDAY

WEDNESDAY

THURSDAY

FRIDAY

SATURDAY

SUNDAY

NOTES

Seven days of fun

MONDAY

TUESDAY

WEDNESDAY

THURSDAY

FRIDAY

SATURDAY

SUNDAY

NOTES

Seven days of fun

MONDAY

TUESDAY

WEDNESDAY

THURSDAY

FRIDAY

SATURDAY

SUNDAY

NOTES

Seven days of fun

MONDAY

TUESDAY

WEDNESDAY

THURSDAY

FRIDAY

SATURDAY

SUNDAY

NOTES

Seven days of fun

MONDAY

TUESDAY

WEDNESDAY

THURSDAY

FRIDAY

SATURDAY

SUNDAY

NOTES

Seven days of fun

MONDAY

TUESDAY

WEDNESDAY

THURSDAY

FRIDAY

SATURDAY

SUNDAY

NOTES

Seven days of fun

MONDAY

TUESDAY

WEDNESDAY

THURSDAY

FRIDAY

SATURDAY

SUNDAY

NOTES

Seven days of fun

MONDAY

TUESDAY

WEDNESDAY

THURSDAY

FRIDAY

SATURDAY

SUNDAY

NOTES

Seven days of fun

MONDAY

TUESDAY

WEDNESDAY

THURSDAY

Weekly Planner

FRIDAY

SATURDAY

SUNDAY

NOTES

Seven days of fun

MONDAY

TUESDAY

WEDNESDAY

THURSDAY

Weekly Planner

FRIDAY

SATURDAY

SUNDAY

NOTES

Seven days of fun

MONDAY

TUESDAY

WEDNESDAY

THURSDAY

FRIDAY

SATURDAY

SUNDAY

NOTES

Seven days of fun

MONDAY

TUESDAY

WEDNESDAY

THURSDAY

FRIDAY

SATURDAY

SUNDAY

NOTES

Seven days of fun

MONDAY

TUESDAY

WEDNESDAY

THURSDAY

Weekly Planner

FRIDAY

SATURDAY

SUNDAY

NOTES

Seven days of fun

MONDAY

TUESDAY

WEDNESDAY

THURSDAY

FRIDAY

SATURDAY

SUNDAY

NOTES

Seven days of fun

MONDAY

TUESDAY

WEDNESDAY

THURSDAY

FRIDAY

SATURDAY

SUNDAY

NOTES

Seven days of fun

MONDAY

TUESDAY

WEDNESDAY

THURSDAY

FRIDAY

SATURDAY

SUNDAY

NOTES

Seven days of fun

MONDAY

TUESDAY

WEDNESDAY

THURSDAY

FRIDAY

SATURDAY

SUNDAY

NOTES

Seven days of fun

MONDAY

TUESDAY

WEDNESDAY

THURSDAY

FRIDAY

SATURDAY

SUNDAY

NOTES

Seven days of fun

MONDAY

TUESDAY

WEDNESDAY

THURSDAY

FRIDAY

SATURDAY

SUNDAY

NOTES

Seven days of fun

MONDAY

TUESDAY

WEDNESDAY

THURSDAY

FRIDAY

SATURDAY

SUNDAY

NOTES

Seven days of fun

MONDAY

TUESDAY

WEDNESDAY

THURSDAY

FRIDAY

SATURDAY

SUNDAY

NOTES

Seven days of fun

MONDAY

TUESDAY

WEDNESDAY

THURSDAY

Weekly Planner

FRIDAY

SATURDAY

SUNDAY

NOTES

Seven days of fun

MONDAY

TUESDAY

WEDNESDAY

THURSDAY

FRIDAY

SATURDAY

SUNDAY

NOTES

Seven days of fun

MONDAY

TUESDAY

WEDNESDAY

THURSDAY

FRIDAY

SATURDAY

SUNDAY

NOTES

Seven days of fun

MONDAY

TUESDAY

WEDNESDAY

THURSDAY

Weekly Planner

FRIDAY

SATURDAY

SUNDAY

NOTES

Seven days of fun

MONDAY

TUESDAY

WEDNESDAY

THURSDAY

FRIDAY

SATURDAY

SUNDAY

NOTES

Seven days of fun

MONDAY

TUESDAY

WEDNESDAY

THURSDAY

Weekly Planner

FRIDAY

SATURDAY

SUNDAY

NOTES

www.ingramcontent.com/pod-product-compliance
Lightning Source LLC
Chambersburg PA
CBHW081336090426
42737CB00017B/3169